MW00964099

I Need You To Know

Words from the Heart for the One I Love

H. Thomas Saylor

FIRST EDITION

Three Dot, L.L.C.
Northville, Michigan

I Need You To Know
Words From the Heart for the One I Love

FIRST EDITION

Library of Congress Control Number: 2004099153

Saylor, H. Thomas, 2004
I Need You To Know: Words From the Heart for the One I Love
ISBN 0-9762012-0-8

a :. **Three Dot, L.L.C.** publication

Three Dot, L.L.C.
143 Cadycentre #339
Northville, Michigan 48167-1433
info@threedotpro.com

book design by Brian Townsend

COVER PHOTO
"Seeds of Love"

The cover photo combines two of the most recognized symbols of culture, religion, spirituality and love. Wheat represents abundance, the fruits of honest and dedicated effort, sustaining nourishment, rebirth and fulfillment. The single rose is given in cherished relationships with yellow signifying joy; pink, perfect happiness; white, purity; and red, the richness and beauty of an everlasting love.

The dormant wheat appears lifeless. When the wheat seed is planted and cultivated, a bountiful harvest follows. So too, words unspoken lie dormant. When words of love are shared and cultivated with loving acts and behaviors, they have the potential to bring forth joy, happiness, purity and lasting love in our relationships.

The three stalks of wheat represent the three words we all long to hear, "I love you." The single rose represents the one true love two dedicated souls can share.

I Need You To Know

We hear the word "love" everywhere.
It is overused and used carelessly. It is used without reverence.
That is why I need you to know something clear and true.

I want you to know when I say, " I love you" it means loyalty.
It means respect. It means devotion.
It means caring. It means acceptance. It means admiration.
It means longing and desire. It means gentle. It means strong.
It means friendship. It means companionship. It means partners.
It means trust. It means alive. It means nonjudgmental.
It means soul mate. It means cherished.
It means assuring. It means solid.
It means unending, without reservation.
It means completely.

So when I say, "I love you," even in one of our hurried moments,
Know, while only a word, it comes from the deepest part of my heart,
A heart full to the brim with reverence, with meaning,
With my belief in you and what we share together.

H. THOMAS SAYLOR

To those who believe in true and lasting love.

*To those in love who desire higher levels of intimacy
and commit to nurturing and growing their relationship.*

To:_____

From:_____

Contents

Introduction

"It is not only necessary to love, it is necessary to say so."
FRENCH PROVERB

We are born into this world seeking love and acceptance. From the moment we take our first breath we cry out for someone to acknowledge our presence, to accept us as we are, to be sensitive to our needs, and to care for us. We are dependent and, for most of us, remain so through our youth. We count on someone to love us, to feed and clothe us, to give us direction and cheer us on.

Then comes the teenage years. It is a time of confusion and uncertainty. Why? It is, because we begin to move toward our independence. We are encouraged to "grow up." We want to grow up and we want to grow up fast. At the same time we are comfortable with being dependent. After all, dependence is what we know. It's safe, warm and comfortable.

Our parents want us to "grow up" too, or so they say. Intellectually they know we need to grow up. God knows, when they look at our messy rooms and pay the bills for clothes and school and books and sports and band they want us to grow up, and they want us to grow up fast. Yet, a dependent relationship with us is what they know too. It's safe, warm and comfortable. When we bring home that first girlfriend or boyfriend, parents are not all that sure they are ready for our independence. No wonder the transition from dependence to independence is such a struggle!

Little by little we move toward independence. We get our degrees. We get our first real jobs. We buy our own cars. We have our own place. We start building a career and an expanded social life. We are climbing and moving and accumulating and networking. We are in charge, making decisions, taking big steps and on the fast track. Yet, with everything so "positive" happening in our lives, what do we long for and share in common? We still find ourselves needing and looking for love.

Yes, most of us are blessed to have the love of family and good friends, and many of us "fall in love" with a special someone. For all our independence, for all our efforts to be on our own, to prove we can make it on our own, we still crave love and acceptance. Like the time of transition from dependence to independence, whether willing to admit it or not, confusion and uncertainty can continue to hover in the background. It can leave us feeling empty, even at a time when our cup looks full to the world around us.

That's what we want the world to believe. The cup is full. See? It's full up to overflowing, and I'm getting an even bigger cup and filling it some more. Will that finally bring us to the safe, warm place of comfort and contentment we long to be? That depends on whether or not we are willing enough and brave enough to move on to interdependence.

Another stage? Yes, another stage. These stages of development are not a new discovery, but a reality well documented and explored by sociologists and philosophers and psychologists and religions. What is amazing is that it remains so foreign to many of us. When we finally arrive at our independence it is hard to even think about making another major shift, but without growing further we will never know the level of fulfillment, satisfaction and completion that is possible in our relationships.

A true story is told about a highly respected and successful scholar, teacher, husband, father and dear friend to many. In his last days, the man was asked what he felt to be most important in life. After all this man had experienced, he came to the conclusion that the greatest challenge and opportunity life holds is learning how to share and to receive love. That is what this book of simple writings is about. It's about learning how to love and be loved. It's about finding ways to say what you feel. It's about the willingness and courage to move beyond independence and into interdependence. It's about surrendering your heart and becoming vulnerable to the one you love. It is about making a decision to accept and embrace someone completely. That is a decision and a change that can happen in an instant but requires a lifetime of dedication and commitment to sustain.

If you make the decision to know true love, choose to nurture the relationship each and every day. There are many ways to do so, but you will find one of the simplest and most rewarding for both of you will be with words. Tell him or her how you feel. Talk to them. Write to them. Be sincere and honest, but don't be afraid to be romantic. Speak in words that might make you feel weak … that show you are surrendering your heart and trusting in the love of your partner. Reminisce about the relationship you have shared. Claim what it can be by describing your vision of the future as if it were real today. Make specific plans to share and enjoy the journey together.

Are there risks with this approach? Yes, as with most things in life, there is risk, but without some risk, is there reward? Is there a chance your words will not be embraced, or appreciated or returned? Perhaps, but the thing to remember is the very real possibility you will connect with your mate in a way the two of you have never known before.

Life is too short to live with regrets and too long to live alone. Move from independence to the fulfillment of interdependence. Make a commitment to change and improve what you personally bring to the relationship. Know the shared private world that can only be discovered by surrendering to the one you love.

Tell them of your love now. Tell them often. Tell them again.

H. THOMAS SAYLOR

Each Petal a Promise

A flower is full of beauty and a rose a bouquet of sweet fragrance,
But a flower remains a flower and a rose a rose
Until given in true love.
When given in love,
Each petal becomes a promise of devotion and commitment,
Full of dreams and hope that last forever ...
A joy that fills the inner places of the heart ...
And gives peace and assurance to friends and lovers true.

13

A Love for All Seasons

I never knew the seasons could be so beautiful.
I never knew sharing a walk in the park could touch me so.
I never expected I'd find the relationship of my dreams,
A love for all seasons,
Then there was you.
As the nights chill and the trees burst into vibrant color ...
My thoughts are of you and your radiance.
So now, as each leaf floats softly to the earth ...
I fall ...
      fall ...
           fall ....
Deeper into our love,
And dreams of resting in your arms forever.

forever

H. THOMAS SAYLOR

Lost and Found

Thinking of you.
Thinking of your smile.
Thinking about losing myself in your eyes.
Giving new meaning to "lost and found!"

The Gift

My heart is filled with memories.
The best ... those I treasure most,
Are the ones you and I made together.
As I relive those moments, I cannot help but think,
Of all the countless precious gifts you have given me.
Those are the gifts I will forever carry with me.
Your love is my ever-present companion ...
My comfort and my reason.
No gift can compare!!!

With that gift you have given me freedom,
The kind of freedom that comes from unconditional love.
It's the freedom that lets me be me.
It's the freedom that lets me dream ...
That lets me speak and feel without judgment ...
Without conditions.

H. THOMAS SAYLOR

freedom

It's the freedom to enjoy being alive ...
The freedom to appreciate the simple things,
And take in the beauty of nature.
You have made me "look up" and truly see the colors of fall,
Feel the gentle kiss of a falling snowflake,
And smell the fragrance of purple lilacs in spring.

Most of all, you have given me
The freedom and the desire to be vulnerable ...
To love completely and without reservation ...
Something that can only exist,
When there will never be another.
You have given me the freedom to love,
To hope and to dream, and you, and you alone,
Make my dreams come true.

You Inspire Me

I want to be more and better for you.
I know I can be selfish.
I jump to conclusions, react before I listen, whine and pout.
I know I have often been insensitive.
The list goes on.
Sadly, I've done it all and in good measure.
Yet, despite my shortcomings, you love me still.
What a gift you are!
All I know is that our love is a true love...
That you are the one and the only one for me.
Knowing that truth makes me more of who I want to be.
Knowing that truth gives me confidence ...
That I can grow just as our love grows.
I am determined to be more of the person you love.
For you ... for us ... I will be the person you need me to be.
You and your perfect love inspire me.

Again and Again

There is no one like you!
You delight me from head to toe!
You fill me up ...
Then surprise and charm me all over again!

again!

Soul Mates

Soul mates are each other's shelter and comfort.
You are mine and I yours.
We are there to listen, to carry the burden,
To lift each other up when the cares of this world weigh heavy.
In this life some rain must fall,
But we face the storms together.
And when the sun comes out,
We dance in the puddles and journey on hand in hand.

dance

Sailing

Sailing through life with you by my side
Takes me exactly where I want to go.
Thank you for making the journey one of joy, of happiness
And hope for our future together.

H. THOMAS SAYLOR

with me
Together

Young love is about being together.
True love is about how much a couple is together even when apart.
You are my one true love.
You are in my heart every moment of every day.
Forever together we will be.

You Are There

There was a time when a cup of coffee was just a cup of coffee ...
When snow was to be shoveled ...
When fall leaves were but a nuisance to be raked ...
When getting up in the morning was a chore ...
When surrounded by others I felt alone ...
When self-doubt tugged at my shirtsleeve,
And tomorrow was but another day.

Then a miracle happened.

a miracle

You walked into my life and a day became an event.
Self-doubt became self-assured.
With you at my side and cradled in my heart I am never alone.
Each day is something to look forward to ...
To live with you ... to explore with you.

H. THOMAS SAYLOR

Leaves are full of color,
Meant to shuffle through on a sunny September day.
Snowflakes silently float down to adorn each branch ...

Trees stand silent... clothed in white ....
Full of life ...
Waiting for the warmth of spring,
Like I wait for the touch of our your hand ...
And the gentle caress of your lips.

Now even a cup of coffee is a comforting reminder of
   caring conversations ...
Of moments shared and inner thoughts revealed ...
Of acceptance ... of trust and commitment ...
Of love freely and completely given and gracefully received.

Yes, there was a time when a cup of coffee was just a cup of coffee.
Now I see you and us and what we have discovered and nurtured together.
In the simplest of things ... in everywhere I go ...
In all that is good and beautiful you are there,
My Miracle, My Dream Come True, My Forever.

The Missing Piece

Born into different worlds,
Missing that elusive something.
Looking for fulfillment in the arms of love,
Needing completion, the missing puzzle piece.

Then you walked into my life.
Now I believe in miracles.
I believe in our world.
Because of you I am whole.
I embrace the day,
And rest assured in our future together.

When We Kiss

When we kiss,
I close my eyes and my heart takes flight.
You are my princess, by lover, my friend, my angel from heaven.
You are my shining star and your kiss my moonlit night.
I am yours forever and for always.

H. THOMAS SAYLOR

Boundless Love

What we share is not bound by time or circumstance.
The sun, moon and stars shine for us.
Our love burns bright and eternal!

burns

bright

Completely

True love is not about taking.
It is not about what you get from a relationship.
No, it is about giving without limits.
It is about receiving love from your partner with grace and gratitude.
You have given such love,
And to you today and for every day to come,
I pledge you my love completely and unconditionally.

Never Let Go

After all this time,
The excitement I felt when our hands first touched and our lips first met
Grows only stronger.
You are my gift, my miracle, my present and my future.
Let's hold on and never let go!

Run to Me

Let me be the one you run to,
The one you confide in,
The one that is there for you
Always and forever.

You Complete Me

You ask, "How does it feel to be completely adored ...
To know that I am the one that completes you?"
Baby, it feels like nothing I have ever known before.
It feels like I am truly accepted as I am
Despite my faults and my shortcomings.
It feels like I can never show you enough how much you mean to me,
And it makes me know one thing for sure.
I will live each day to love you, to try to show you,
To give to you all that my heart and soul can offer.
You are my best friend, my lover and my everything.
Know you are indeed "desired irresistibly."
You are the essence of life that makes me whole.

My Pledge to You

Nothing will ever change the way I feel about you.
Absolutely nothing.
Not time. Not space.
Not where we live or where we go or whom we are with.
Not fear or jealously.
Not my ego or my selfish thoughts.
Not my insecurities or the problems of life.
Nor what is said or not said.
I pledge you my undying love,
For always and a day.

always

Forever Love

Whatever life brings,
Whatever changes or complications,
Whatever demands we face,
Whatever clock marks our time,
Whatever life brings,
My love for you is forever.

More Than Ever

The stress and challenges of the day
May sometimes be a lot to bear,
But know this.
I love you more than ever,
Not with limits, but with my whole being.
I cherish you and what we have.
You are the best thing that has ever come into my life.

come into

my life

One-gether

Our love is strong and resilient,
Enduring and real, growing and supportive ...
A living promise between two soul mates.
I will always be there when you call.
I will live the promises made.
"Onegether" we will open new doors
And find caring ways to nurture our love in our world.

H. THOMAS SAYLOR

Run Away with Me

Run away with me to our world!
Let's explore today together.
Let's talk and laugh and embrace.
Let's share out ups and downs,
Our work, our play.
Let's explore our past together!
Let's talk and laugh and embrace.
Let's relive our special moments.
Our youth, our private yesterdays.
Let's dream our future together!
Let's talk and laugh and embrace.
Let's release our worries and reveal our hopes.
Our wants, our desires.
Run away with me to our world and
Love as no others have ever loved before.

Thank You

Thank you for the smiles you bring.
Thank you for all you do.
Thank you for all the big things ...
And all the little things;
For your caring and your patience,
For your acceptance and understanding,
For your encouragement and support,
For all the laughter and conversation,
For all the dreaming and remembering,
Thank you for all the smiles.
For all the memories;
For heartfelt promises and hope.
For that look and gentle elbow,
For eyes that sparkle,
For words spoken and unspoken,
For all the big things,
And all the little things,
Thank you for making me smile.

H. THOMAS SAYLOR

Ever More

As the days and years go by
My admiration,
My desire,
And my heart and soul-felt love
For the precious one you are,
Continue to grow.
Because of your friendship,
Your openness and sharing,
And all your nurturing ways ...
I can't help but love you more.

love you
more

Privilege

If I could have only one wish ... one dream ...
It would be that I might have the privilege,
Yes, the privilege, to have you in my life forever.
So know whatever the years may bring,
Whatever circumstance throws our way,
There is nothing, absolutely nothing,
That will keep me from loving you,
My dream come true.

Honey Sweet

You give me the gift of friendship, of hope,
And the thrill of unconditional love.
You give me the true joy of waking up each day
To the honey sweet reality of having you in my life!

H. THOMAS SAYLOR

Longing

I close my eyes and see your face.
We draw near.
I reach out my hand to touch your cheek of silk.
I sense the warmth of your breath and crave the taste of your kiss.
I long to be where you are.

where

you are

Until Then

If I cannot be held by you, I need not be held.
If I cannot be touched by you, I wish not to be touched.
If I cannot be kissed by you, I yearn for no other.

Until we can embrace ...
Until I feel your caress ...
Until our lips meet again ...
I will be content in the memories of our world,
And the promise of your love.

You Take My Breath Away

There are few things more beautiful than a rose, but you ...
You put the rose to shame.
Your beauty takes my breath away.

beauty

Consumed

I cannot wait until you are in my arms again.
I close my eyes and dream of your soft skin,
Your sweet fragrance,
Your breath caressing my cheek.
I am consumed by the thought of your kiss,
And the very instant your lips first touch mine.

You Fill My Heart

Thank you for choosing to walk with me.
It is with you I find happiness and hope.
It is because of you my heart is filled.
It is in you that I find what makes me whole.
I am yours, every step of the way.

walk
with me

Holding Hands

I had never really thought about holding hands until there was you.
Now I find myself anticipating what has become an intimate connection.
Like your kiss, a gift always appreciated and never taken for granted.
Our hands touch and the energy of love flows.
I sense how our fingers intertwine and how your skin feels.
I am conscious of your movements and your grasp.
I think of how perfectly we fit together and know,
You and I were meant to be.

meant

My Destination

Sometimes you don't know how lost you are,
Until you arrive at an unexpected place.
I was lost ... so very lost.
But fate intervened, and I discovered you!
In you I found my destination.
In you I have purpose and passion, and I know one defining truth.
I was meant to love you,
Completely ... forever ... and beyond!

to be

You!

Life.
Moment after moment strung together.
Most go unnoticed much less remembered.
But you!
The slightest touch of your hand,
The look in your eyes,
The tenderness of your kiss,
The caress of your cheek against my face,
Makes each moment with you
A precious and lasting assurance
Of our steadfast love!

Time Together

I wish our times together would never end.
That's what happens when true love bonds two meant only for each other.
The quality of what we share is beyond words ... beyond measure!
We have a love so satisfying, so complete,
That the time spent together will never, ever be enough.

H. THOMAS SAYLOR

Becoming One

First there was you,
And then there was me.
One day a meeting ...
And then there were we.
Then you became you and I became me,
And soon there was one
Forever to be!

41

measure

Fun

Fun.
Spontaneous. Energizing. Engaging fun.
Smiles unlimited.
Freedom to be, to play, to express, to enjoy.
No judgment. No criticism.
Acceptance and respect.

Children know how to have fun.
Remember?
We didn't have to plan it or arrange it.
We didn't have to shape it or control it.
Fun happened, and we knew it would be.
Magically the right ingredients were just there ...
And in the right proportions.

Sometimes we forget how to have fun.
Sometimes life creates barriers.
Sometimes circumstance drains the fun right out of us.
It happens over time and one may not even realize that it is missing.
I had lost fun.

Then I met you!
Spontaneous! Energizing! Engaging!
Freedom to be ... to play ... to express ... to enjoy!
No judgments. Acceptance and respect. Smiles unlimited.
Magically the right ingredients in the right proportion.

When I am with you fun happens, and I know it will always be.
No matter what we do or where we go,
Life will be fun together!

Thank you for all you are and all you give, and thank you for the gift of fun!

engaging

The Perfect Couple

Don't we make the perfect couple?
The magic of true love transforms our relationship
    into all that is beautiful ...
Full of grace and peace
And heartfelt confidence in our private world.

Happy Birthday

When I think of important dates in my life, your birthday is at the very top.
It was on this date that you, My Beloved, began the journey in life.
It was then that destiny began day-by-day bringing us together.
All the experiences along the way,
All the smiles and frowns,
All the good times and difficult ones too,
Have helped shape you into the unique person you are today.
You are the one I fell head-over-heals in love with ...
The person I fall deeper for with every breath I take.
I adore each and every facet of who you are ...
And I do mean every part ... exactly how you are.

I Promise You

I search for the words,
But words fail to express the joy you have brought into my life.
I can only promise you my undying love and devotion
And a heart full of gratitude
For you and what we share together.

_we share
together_

45

My Precious Gift

Of all my experiences in life,
Of all the people I have ever met,
Of all the family and friends that I have known,
Of all that I have possessed or ever will,
You are my most precious gift!
You are truly my everything and my greatest delight!
I will love you with all that I have forever and beyond.

forever

More!

It's so hard to say, "goodbye," even for a day.
Everything about you screams
Beautiful ... sensual ... stylish ... classy ... delicious!
I can't wait for more!

H. THOMAS SAYLOR

Your Happiness Is My Joy

While I know I am far from perfect,
I hope and pray that you are able
To feel the true love and devotion I have for you.
For there is no greater joy than your happiness
And the opportunity to share life with you,
The love of my life and the fulfillment of my dreams.

47

and
beyond

True Intimacy

There was a time when I didn't know what intimacy meant.
In my youth, I may not have known the word existed.
I had a few important friendships, but relationships came and went.
Something was missing.
Life seemed to be going by so fast.
Seemed like I was going to miss out.
Felt like I needed to move ahead ...
Like I needed to get somewhere or be left behind.
I was so anxious about the future
That I didn't listen to the voice inside that said, "all in God's time."

While blessed in so many ways throughout my life,
I never found the closeness that I desired ...
Until I found you.
The same voice that told me to be patient, told me to surrender to you.
This time I listened!
It is in that complete surrender,
I finally found the intimacy I had for so long yearned.
You are my soul mate and my confidant,
My joy ... my trust from heaven.
I will love you eternally,
My delight,
My sweetest vision come true.

H. THOMAS SAYLOR

My Winter Love

A fresh dusting of white snow covered the ground
As children's laughter stirred memories of long ago.
We walked among the angels hand in hand,
And there on the edge of the frozen lake we embraced ...
Never to let go, my winter love and I,
Never to let go.

never let go

You're the One

As I sat beside you,
All I could think about was how fulfilled and how content you make me.
How can I ever convey the depth of that feeling?
The truth is, while I will never cease to try, no words suffice.
But what I can do, and will do, is love you in a caring and gentle way.
What I can do is promise you my devotion,
Then live that promise without hesitation.
I can live with gratitude and joy in my heart.
I can give myself to you totally.
I can assure you that there is but one love of my life,
And you, My Darling, are the one.

My Very Breath

I cannot express in words or deeds the love I have for you
Or the gratefulness I feel in my heart.
You are my breath of life!
You make life worth living!
You satisfy my every need and desire!

H. THOMAS SAYLOR

darling

Love Satisfies

Each day with you is a gift.
Your smile warms my heart …
Your eyes captivate my thoughts …
And the touch of your hand assures me of your promises.
The caress of your kiss awakens every passion within me,
And your love, and only your love,
Satisfies my every longing.

Here For You

Sometimes life can be so unsettling ...
So full of change and uncertainty.
That is why I want to affirm something that will not change ...
Something you can count on.
Please accept my continued and ever stronger commitment to loving you.
My loyalty, my desire to give myself completely will not waiver.
I am here for you.
I will always be here for you.
You are my one true love, my passion, my oasis.
What I give to you, and I give my all, I offer willingly and with joy.
There is nothing ever to fear.
Just let me be the one to love you.
Let me be yours,
And you will know love steadfast and true.

52
—

I Know

While miles come between us,
I know from moments past,
Out love is never ending!
Forever it will last!

Stay With Me

It's true! You are the one I have been looking for all of my life!
I just didn't know your name or where to find you.
But now ... now that we have found each other ...
Now that you and I have become us ...
Now, that the one meant for me is in my arms,
I will never, ever, ever, let go!
Stay with me, My Love.
Let's dream together and make those dreams come true.
Let's live this perfect reality to our very last breath!

dream

Always True

When I think of promises,
I think of you.
I think of secrets shared,
Of happiness found,
Of real moments destined to last forever in our hearts.
I think of our commitment to each other and know,
I will always be true.

The Perfect Card

When I go to the card shop,
I search to find just the right one for you ... for us.
I read card after card.
I think about the words.
Do they somehow capture the tender moments in our world?
It is for those moments together I live.
I cherish every second.
Every time your hand is in mine ...
Every time out eyes meet ...
Every time our lips touch,
Is another moment in paradise.

H. THOMAS SAYLOR

Let's Dance

The pleasure of walking next to you,
The beauty of sunlight on your face,
The exhilaration I know when I am with you ...
Makes me feel like dancing!

paradise

My Music

I enjoy music.
I enjoy music of all kinds.
Sometimes it doesn't matter what is playing.
At other times, I like the tune to fit my mood.
Upbeat and loud at times.
At others, slow and mellow.
Sometimes pop, sometimes rock, a little classic for good measure,
And sometimes only jazz will do.
As I drive down the road the radio buttons are kept busy,
The CDs are cycling,
And some of my old favorite tapes are at hand.
You just can't find the right music for all occasions,
For every mood and situation at one place on the dial.

But when it comes to my happiness,
I don't have to push buttons or change CDs.
I don't have to search for what fits the mood of the day.
I don't have to look for something new because I've grown tired of the old.
All I need is to think of you.
All I need is to have you near.
All I need is you in my life.

You are my music for all occasions.
You are the song that is perfect for every mood, every desire, every need.
You, and you alone, are my favorite melody!

H. THOMAS SAYLOR

Trust

You wonder if I trust you?
Truth is, I've never thought about mistrusting you.
Not because I take anything we share for granted,
But because your love for me is so reassuring, so warm, so caring.
How could I but trust you completely?

Loving You So

Loving you is so rewarding,
So fulfilling, so uplifting,
So energizing, so beautiful,
So easy, so joyful,
And so so so so so much fun!
I never get enough of you!

Passion Ablaze

Every time we make love,
The passion and desire I feel for you intensifies.
You never cease to amaze me ... to surprise and delight me!
You put out the fire and start a new blaze all at the same time!

True Love Found

You fill every void in my life.
My heart, my love and my devotion are yours alone.
I've found the true meaning of love in you.

and delight

My Miracle

You are my miracle.
You have brought happiness and hope into my life ...
Like I have never known before,
Greater than I could have ever imagined.
Only you can complete me.
Only you fulfill my every yearning.

59

When You Are Happy

I am happiest when you are happy.
When you are smiling, when you are content,
When your worries are not a burden ...
Then I too am smiling and content.
So know that what pleases you pleases me,
That your dreams are my dreams,
That your desires are but opportunities for me ...
To show my love for you.

As I Am

You inspire me.
You don't try to change me.
You don't judge me or manipulate me.
You don't use me or take advantage.
No, you bring out a side of me that I want to be for you ... for us.
I don't have to change who I am, or what I like,
Or pretend my opinions conform to yours.
You take me as I am.
That makes my desire to make you happy even greater ...
To be there for you ...
To truly and completely love you.

belong

Where I Belong

You fill my thoughts.
You fill my heart.
I hear your voice.
I see your face.
I'm lost in your eyes and found again,
Because with you I am right where I belong.

61

Anticipation

While we have not been able to spend much time together lately,
Nothing can touch the love I feel for you.
It still grows stronger by the moment.
Just knowing that you are near and that you love me too,
Warms my heart ...
And builds anticipation of our sweet tomorrows.

Soon

Soon we will be together.
Soon we will be in each other's arms.
Soon our lips will meet.
Soon we will exchange words of love and comfort.
Soon.

Your Search is Over

If you are looking for someone who cares for you in every way,
Appreciates your love and all you do,
Dreams of you and your "ways,"
Likes you exactly as you are,
Sees only a lasting love,
Respects you, your opinions and accomplishments,
Doesn't want to change you,
Adores you,
Keeps you in their thoughts,
Trusts you and believes in you,
Holds you gently in their heart,
Considers you their best and dearest friend ...
And loves you more and more each day,
Then, Baby, you've come to the right place!

My Pleasure

It is such a pleasure to love you,
To give my heart to you,
To hold you gently in my thoughts.

Captivating

I just wanted you to know how captivating you are!
You face is radiant.
Your eyes sparkle.
The happiness and enthusiasm in your voice ...
Makes me warm and excited inside.
You make me feel loved and refreshed ...
Anxious to spend every possible moment with you.

Let Me Please You

I feel the deepest passion for you.
I desire you beyond description.
I want to please you in every way …
Make you squirm with delight.
I am yours in all ways,
In any way,
For this and every day.

Can You Hear the Music?

Listen.
Can you hear the music?
Can you hear the melody of my love for you?
It's strong but not too loud.
It's gentle but not too soft.
It plays without ceasing ...
Meant only for you.

Every treasure

Every moment a gift.
Every word a song.
Every meeting a treasure.

H. THOMAS SAYLOR

Hold On Tight

Life takes us to some unknown places ...
To valleys low and mountains high.
We think we know where we are going,
Yet roads confuse.
We wonder, "Why?"
In you, I found the unexpected ....
Someone to help me find my way.
A warm smile and understanding,
For you I'm thankful every day.
So take my hand and walk beside me.
Please hold on tight.
I need you there.
With our love and our friendship,
As one we'll journey,
No matter where.

Prepared to Love

If I have any regrets in life, it's that we weren't born in the same town ...
To families who lived in the same neighborhood.
That way, I could have known you all my life.
I could have grown up with my best friend,
Chased you around the playground,
Built a snowman and made snow angels together.

You see, until there was you, I existed,
But was not truly alive.
Until there was you,
I was not whole.
Until there was you in my life,
I had no idea what was missing.

Maybe it is because of what we did not know in our past,
That allows us to appreciate the present ...
To be the best of friends ...
To unconditionally like each other as we do.
Besides ...
I think there is still time ...
To chase you through the park and play in the snow together, don't you?
Let's make the most of every moment shared!

H. THOMAS SAYLOR

Because of You

Each day is a new joy for me because of you.
You make me smile.
You give me strength.
You are my true north, my hope and my forever best friend.
You make memories precious and bring promise to the future.

Imagine

Imagine for a minute that we had never met.
Ready?
One thousand one, one thousand two, one thousand three,
    one thousand ...
STOP!
That is far too painful to continue!
Let's contemplate instead the miracle we have found in each other.
Now that is something to think about every day of our lives!

It's Your Love

It's your love that warms my soul,
That makes me whole,
That opens my heart and lets me be me.
It's your love that I'm so grateful for,
That I anticipate, that gives me hope and makes real moments possible.
It's the kind of love that only best friends and lovers share ...
That is always there for me.
What a treasure you are!
I will never, ever take your precious love for granted.

I Never Knew

I never knew real moments like ours,
So special,
So warm and true,
Until I put my hand in yours ...
Then life began brand new!

H. THOMAS SAYLOR

my heart

Something to Count On

While some things in life are a gamble, my love is not.
You can count on it like money in the bank ...
Like the sun, moon and stars.
Fixed.
Firm.
Ever present.
Like a rock.
Etched in stone reality.

Lost in Love

When I look into your eyes, I become lost in my love for you.
We connect on so many levels,
And the excitement of sharing the future with you is beyond words!
You are the love of my life!
The joy of my existence!

At First Sight

Love at first sight?
It is possible.
You and I know it can be.
But, what about friendship at first sight?
Perhaps not, because friendship is a process.
It grows from a base of mutual interest and concern.
It is nurtured by shared experience ...
By a true appreciation for each other's need to be listened to,
To be supported and comforted.
That growing relationship is held together by trust and acceptance,
And, in our case, love.
I have always valued our friendship,
But now, knowing what we have,
It has become a crowning jewel for which I love you even more.

friendship

H. THOMAS SAYLOR

Our Real Moment

Our real moment is endless.
There is so much to cherish,
But oh so much yet to be discovered and experienced together.
And, while we are remembering and planning and doing ...
We will be "one-gether."
That union is the intimacy ...
The inseparable bond in our relationship ...
I will for always hold dear.

73

Your Love a Treasure

Your love is a treasure.
How you care for me and show concern for me ...
How you tease me and peak my curiosity ...
How you nurture our relationship and keep each day refreshing and new.
Your openness and sharing ...
Your kindness ...
The gentle way you hold my heart ...
Your courage to try something different,
And the romantic way you take us places ...
Your willingness to sometimes lead and sometimes follow,
And your knack for knowing what is just right for the occasion.
Well, I could go on and on and on about my love for you,
And you know what?
In our lifetime together, I intend to do just that!

Images

When together, I can never get enough of you.
When apart, I long to hold you in my arms.
When alone, sweet memories and images ...
Images of what can and will be ...
Bring us closer than others in love will ever know.

True Love Grows

The love I feel for you is boundless.
It grows every day.
It brings me joy and strength,
Hope and certainty,
Happiness in the present …
And anticipation of our bright future together.

together

I Know Love

When I am with you I know.
I know love ... a love of many textures.
Love ... smooth as silk.
Love ... warm as the fist sip of cocoa on a cold winter's day.
I know where I want to be.
I know the person I want to be with.
I know love pure and honest ... spun gold ...
Moon beams ... petals soft and fragrant.
When I am with you I know.
I know love and I know I love you.

My Fulfillment

You draw me in.
I yearn to touch you.
You own my inner thoughts.
You are my reality, my fantasy ...
The fulfillment of my longings.

H. THOMAS SAYLOR

Sail On Together

She called him "Sailor."
He called her "Dreamboat."
Both enjoyed the beauty and allure of the water,
And, while neither new how to sail,
It became a symbol of their desire to be together,
To be at peace with life ... together ... as one.
No, sailing had never bee a part of their past,
But the same winds of destiny that brought them together,
Now fill their souls and carry them on,
Hand in hand,
To uncharted islands known only to them.

True Love

True love looks beyond and anew.
True love embraces the beautiful and cherishes the whole.
True love is not blind but makes a choice,
To stand where sunlight brightens,
And let all that is good shine through.

Perfect Harmony

Our hearts sing in perfect harmony.
We are drawn together by the bond of true love.
Knowing no bounds.
Endless.
An enchanting melody of pure tone,
Filled with hope and promise and longing anticipation.

H. THOMAS SAYLOR

In an Instant

Isn't it funny how when something is lost ...
You can search and search but never find what you are looking for?
Then, when you least expect it, something shiny catches your eye.
You're in the right place at the right time.
In an instant that will never repeat,
The light is just right,
The angle is just so,
And a reflection makes you look up.
Suddenly you see what might have been lost forever.

Thank you for shining in my life.
Thank you for revealing your love to me.
Now, the only thing I cannot find are the words ...
The words to describe all that is in my heart for you.

Our Destiny

It is so hard to believe that in the ocean of life,
Two seemingly lost ships, crossed paths.
Now one ship, our ship, sails on,
Discovering joy and adventure,
Sharing rainbows,
Charting one course.
For us, there are no boundaries and no end to our journey.
So come, travel with me.
There are sunsets to chase and stars to count.
It is our time.
It is our destiny.

My Special Gift

Here I sit waiting for you, feeling like a kid on Christmas morning.
But you ... you are a very special gift.
You're not the kind wrapped in colored paper and bows.
No, you are wrapped in beauty and radiance.
As each precious facet of who you are is revealed,
I love you even more.

H. THOMAS SAYLOR

Searching

Searching.
Two hearts longing.
Two souls incomplete.
Traveling through life on parallel roads yet destined to cross.
Separated by circumstance.
Reaching out. Joining hands. Embracing.
Building bridges meant only for the two of us to cross.
Becoming one.
Whole at last.
Forever.

in radiance

On the Road

The room is cold and worn. The noise of the city fills the air.
If only you were here. If only you were beside me.
We would warm the night.
We would talk and laugh and look into each other's eyes.
We would share the passion that consumes.
But wait. There is something familiar in this room.
It gives me comfort and lifts my spirit.
How could I forget?
You sent your love along.

Fate Fulfilled

Look into my eyes.
See deep within my thoughts.
Sense what I'm feeling.
Touch my hand.
Experience the connection … a confirmation of fate fulfilled.
Feel the strength, the embrace, the hope
That comes only from knowing you are truly loved.

Our Star Burns Bright

Artists will paint their images and poets will craft their words,
Yet none will know what we have known or feel what we have felt.
No one has.
No one will.
For where our hearts meet a new light shines.
There, our star burns bright ...
With splendor known only to you and I.

feeling

Time Stands Still

In your arms time stands still.
In your eyes, I am lost forever.

You Are

You are ...
My friend,
My keepsake,
My gift,
My love,
My greatest blessing!

H. THOMAS SAYLOR

My Artist

If not a poet, how do you give simple words new meaning?
If not a musician, why do songs now play just for you and I?
If not a sculptor, how do you shape my thoughts and aspirations?
So share with me, my Dear One, your poems, your melodies, your images.
Fill me with the beauty that is you ... that only you create.

create

85

Time

Time can be an enemy,
But remember, it was time and destiny that brought us together.
Hold on to our memories,
Until we are once again making new ones together.

Love Blooms Fresh

Time and space may separate,
But true love is not bound by circumstance.
True love blooms fresh each day.
Its fragrance fills our souls,
So we can always be united.

Destiny

Destiny brought us together at the right moment in time.
We wish we had met long before,
But it is our past that has prepared us for our future.
It is our past that has enabled us ...
To appreciate the richness of what we share.

each day

When We Are Apart

The days apart are long, but our memories are sweet.
Hold on to good thoughts and know,
My dreams are of you.
They are of you and only you.

My Silent Song

Amid the noise and confusion a silent song plays for you.
It's a song of my love,
A sweet melody,
Meant only for your heart to hear.

All Things New

When words of love are shared,
Even the simple things in life take on new significance.

dearest

My Dearest Friend

It is impossible to adequately describe the meaning of our friendship.
All I know is that I can never get enough of you ...
Your laughter ... your caring ... your unassuming conversation.

H. THOMAS SAYLOR

I See Your Face

When alone, I close my eyes and see your face.
My mind wanders through the memories we have created.
I smile.
Sometimes I laugh aloud.
Once in a while I shed a tear.
Not a tear of sadness,
But an expression of gratitude for having you in my life.
Thank you for making all things new!

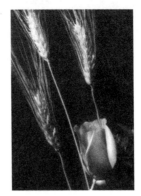

Our Journey Together

Come travel life's road with me. Take my hand, so if we ever lose our way,
we will never lose each other.

There are three Greek words that describe the essential components of true love. The words are *agape*, *phileo*, and *eros*. *Agape* refers to the commitment and duty we vow to our relationship. *Phileo* is the emotional component that describes the affection, friendship and sense of care we feel for our partner. *Eros* love is the physical component. It is the sexual expression of our love. These three elements are themes reflected in the preceding pages and ones this journal can reinforce.

Why a journal? Because giving thoughtful and honest consideration of the topics, especially if done as a couple, will facilitate dialogue. Writing down those thoughts will reinforce your commitment and create a record for future reflection. Sharing fond memories, showing appreciation for your mate and planning for your future together will strengthen your desire to nurture your relationship. It can also help you "hold on" to your mate as you experience the inevitable "bumps" in life's road. Talk about those "bumps" when they happen, and assure your partner of your commitment to see things through with them at your side.

The journal touches on the three essential components of true love. If used in the spirit intended it should increase your empathy for the needs of the one you love. It is vital that we express and demonstrate our love, and it is critical that each of us be sensitive to the love needs of our partner.

However you choose to use the journal, take it seriously, but have fun with it. Don't make it a task to rush through and check off the "to do" list. Take time with it. Trade it back and forth with your significant other, and add a note or comment each time you do. Block out an hour or two of uninterrupted time. Turn off the television, cell phones and other distractions. Take a half hour to reminisce, and build a list of your favorite memories. Then come up with at least one thing each of you would like to do together in the coming weeks. Keep a calendar handy and schedule time to make your plans a reality. End each session by sharing something you sincerely appreciate about the other. If you do, you might just find yourself enjoying the third component of love more often and more fully.

It's all about who you're with, Babe,
and, Babe, I'm with you!

I enjoy being with you because ...

_____

_____

_____

_____

_____

_____

94

_____

_____

_____

_____

_____

_____

_____

_____

H. THOMAS SAYLOR

In all my days,
There has never been anything or anyone as attractive to me as you.
You thrill me!

Some of the many qualities that attract me to you are ...

_____

_____

_____

_____

_____

_____

95

_____

_____

_____

_____

_____

_____

_____

You are the center of my thoughts.
You are the stars of my sky.
You are the very beat of my heart.

When I think about you I imagine ...

_____

_____

_____

_____

_____

_____

96

_____

_____

_____

_____

_____

_____

_____

My favorite place to be is next to you!
We were made for each other, Sweetheart.
Let's walk through life side by side.

Remember the time we ...

_____

_____

_____

_____

_____

_____

_____

97

_____

_____

_____

_____

_____

_____

_____

One gentle brush of your lips on mine ...
Moves me more ...
Than the sum of all the affection I have ever known before.

Our kisses are oh so good! I love it when you kiss me ...

You know of my favorite places and favorite things,
But you are my favorite of all favorites!

Let's make plans to ...

_____

_____

_____

_____

_____

_____

_____

_____

_____

_____

_____

_____

_____

_____

Hand in hand we will discover all that can be
for friends and lovers true.

Experiences I would like to share with you include ...

_____

_____

_____

_____

_____

_____

100

_____

_____

_____

_____

_____

_____

_____

H. THOMAS SAYLOR

When we share music, we share love.
When you shared your heart,
You wrote our song forever in my soul.

Among the songs that have special meaning to our relationship are ...

_____

_____

_____

_____

_____

_____

_____

_____

_____

_____

_____

_____

_____

_____

Each day I marvel at the total person you are
and the miracle of your love.
You captivate my heart and live within my soul.

I may never have told you this before, but I marvel at the way you ...

_____

_____

_____

_____

_____

_____

102
___

_____

_____

_____

_____

_____

_____

_____

_____

My joy! My passion! My miracle!
You take my breath away and
breathe life into my heart!

I remember times when I felt really down. You were there to give me comfort and hope when ...

_____

_____

_____

_____

_____

_____

_____

_____

_____

_____

_____

_____

_____

_____

When we are apart, I carry you in my heart.
When we are together again, life begins anew!

When we are apart I think about ...

_____

_____

_____

_____

_____

_____

_____

_____

_____

_____

_____

_____

_____

_____

H. THOMAS SAYLOR

In your eyes I see all that is good and beautiful.
In your arms I long to rest forever.

When I look into your eyes ...

_____

_____

_____

_____

_____

_____

_____

105

_____

_____

_____

_____

_____

_____

_____

The sweetness of your love never leaves me.
Thinking of you constantly.

Because I love you so, I want to ...

_____

_____

_____

_____

_____

_____

_____

_____

_____

_____

_____

_____

_____

_____

_____

H. THOMAS SAYLOR

How sweet it is to surrender all my love to you!
Our love is beyond all measure!

Let's nurture our love and continue to grow closer by ...

_____

_____

_____

_____

_____

_____

_____

_____

_____

_____

_____

_____

_____

_____

A Look in the Mirror

Love is patient, love is kind. It does not envy, it does not boast, it is not proud.
It is not rude, it is not self–seeking, it is not easily angered, it keeps no record of wrongs.
Love does not delight in evil but rejoices with the truth. It always protects, always trusts,
always hopes, always perseveres. Love never fails.

I COR.13: 4 − 8

One of the toughest steps each of us must take in order to grow personally and in our relationships is to take an honest look in the mirror. This is especially true at a time in our culture when career, material goods and the expectation for immediate gratification can consume too much of our attention. There is a lot of talk about achieving "work/life balance," but many of us end up trying to force a bit of "life" into our work instead of building a life based on values and priorities.

Life balance is multi-dimensional. It includes the spiritual, physical, psychological, educational, social, vocational and avocational. This book is not intended to be a guide to achieving life balance. For that, I encourage you to take advantage of the many caring and capable relationship professionals available through your church and in your community.

Whether reading this book for your own pleasure, giving it to someone you love, or receiving it as a gift please consider both the beauty and the challenge contained in the above quote. The words may sound familiar as they are often spoken at weddings and written in greeting cards. Don't we all desire to be loved in that way? The words are beautiful indeed, but if you really consider what they say, it is also a challenge. It describes a very high standard for our attitudes, thoughts and behaviors.

This definition of love serves as a meaningful benchmark when we look in the mirror. Keep in mind our individual responsibility in the nurturing process. Our individual role is to change and improve how we personally give love and how we accept love. It is to encourage positive personal change and positive growth in the relationship. It is not about how to make your partner change. If you set out to change her or him, you may not get the results you are looking for. Relationships are like investments. They take time and frequent deposits, but if one is faithful in following a sound investment plan the rewards can be greater than ever imagined.

The following sample questions are intended to help identify opportunities for growth. This is a private and personal reflection exercise, so be completely honest. Don't be discouraged if the answers are not always what you would like. You are not alone. Remember, you should feel good about your desire to grow, and as you take steps to plant seeds of love in your relationship, you are more likely to experience the love and interdependence you are seeking.

Sample Questions

Do I accept responsibility for my actions and the success of my relationship?

Are my expectations set at a reasonable and appropriate level?

When I fail or offend the one I love, do I say that I am sorry? Do I express sincere remorse and my desire to change? Do I take steps to change?

Do I regularly ask my mate about their day, hopes and dreams? Do I then listen to their answers without interrupting, judgment or telling them what to do?

How does the level of courtesy and respect I show to the one I love compare to what I would show toward my most important business client?

Do I regularly make time to spend with my mate to do the things she or he enjoys?

Am I slow to anger, or do I frequently respond with a raised voice or critical comment?

Do I see and acknowledge the good in him or her?

Does my body language suggest a positive attitude, or do I purposefully or unconsciously use my body language to criticize or disapprove?

Do I express appreciation for qualities in my mate?

Am I sensitive to my mate's worries, needs and desires?

Do I take joy in the achievements and successes of the one I love?

Are romantic gestures something I offer throughout the year or only on anniversaries and holidays?

Do I give my mate space and help her or him find time to do the things they enjoy? Do I do so without judgment or demands?

Am I able to forgive and put away old wrongs?

Can I list my true love's favorite things?

Have I chosen to trust my mate?

Do the things I own interfere with the relationship I desire?

Am I financially and morally responsible in my relationship?

When there are disappointments and difficult times along the way, do I remain hopeful, confident and willing to persevere?

Do I share the same value system with my mate? Are my faith and beliefs a priority?

Am I kind and considerate? Do I demonstrate the level of concern and politeness that was evident early in our relationship?

When there are disagreements, do I dwell on my partner's mistakes or focus on my own?

Do I bring up old wounds?

Do I frequently talk about my accomplishments, needs and plans, or do I first take interest in the accomplishments, needs and plans of the one I love?

Must I always be in control of the situation?

What are my priorities in life? Do my actions reflect my priorities?

Do I look for ways and take action to lessen the burdens that weigh on my mate?

Day in and day out, do I treat the one I love in the same ways I wish to be treated and cared for?

Am I aware of the three components of true love, and do I consider that my mate's needs in each of those areas may be different than my own? Am I sensitive to her or his love needs and respond accordingly?

HOW TO ORDER

To order additional copies of this book or other **Three Dot** publications, please contact your local bookseller or gift store, order by mail using the coupon below, or e-mail **info@threedotpublications.com**.

TO ORDER BY MAIL*

Clip and mail this coupon, along with check or money order payable to:

Three Dot, L.L.C.
143 Cadycentre #339
Northville, Michigan 48167-1119

✂ -

I Need You to Know

Number of copies	____ @ $9.95 U.S.	$_____.__
	____ @ $14.95 CAN.	_____.__
Michigan Residents add 6% Sales Tax		_____.__
Plus shipping and handling per copy in the U. S. ____ @ $3.00		_____.__
Or per copy for shipment to Canada ____ @ $5.00 CAN.		_____.__

TOTAL ENCLOSED PAYABLE TO: THREE DOT, L.L.C. $_____.__

SHIPPING INFORMATION:

Name _____

Address _____

_____

City _____ State/Province _____ Zip _____

*30-day money-back guarantee. Allow 3-6 weeks for delivery.